Reading Roundabout

Seeing

Paul Humphrey

Photography by Chris Fairclough

W
FRANKLIN WATTS
LONDON•SYDNEY

First published in 2007 by
Franklin Watts
338 Euston Road
London NW1 3BH

Franklin Watts Australia
Level 17/207 Kent Street
Sydney NSW 2000

ISBN: 978 0 7496 7449 6 (hbk)
ISBN: 978 0 7496 7461 8 (pbk)

Dewey classification number: 612.8'4

A CIP catalogue record for this book is available from the British Library.

Planning and production by Discovery Books Limited
Editor: Rachel Tisdale
Designer: Ian Winton
Photography: Chris Fairclough
Series advisors: Diana Bentley MA and Dee Reid MA,
Fellows of Oxford Brookes University

The author, packager and publisher would like to thank the following
people for their participation in this book: Auriel and Ottilie Austin-Baker,
Bryn Stallard-Pearson, Harriet and Imogen Stanley, Lucas Tisdale,
the students and teachers of Penn Hall School, Wolverhampton.

All photographs by Chris Fairclough except for the following:
P9: Tony Dilger; P19: The Guide Dogs for the Blind Association.

Printed in China

Franklin Watts is a division of Hachette Children's Books, an Hachette Livre UK company.

Community Learning & Libraries
Cymuned Ddysgu a Llyfrgelloedd

This item should be returned or renewed by the last date stamped below.

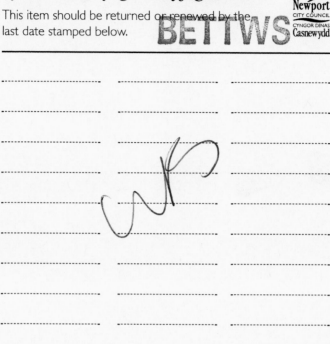

BETTWS

Newport
CITY COUNCIL
CYNGOR DINAS
Casnewydd

To renew telephone: 656656 or 656657 (minicom) or www.newport.gov.uk/libraries

ENRICHING
LEARNING IN
NEWPORT
SCHOOLS

Contents

Five senses

You have five senses. They are seeing, touching, hearing, smelling and tasting.

Touching

Seeing

Hearing

Smelling

Tasting

5

Look at your eyes

The black dot in the middle of your eye is your pupil.

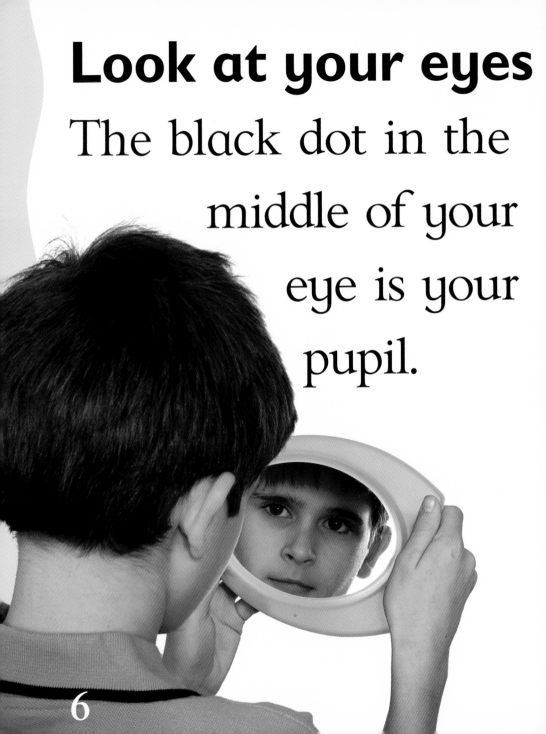

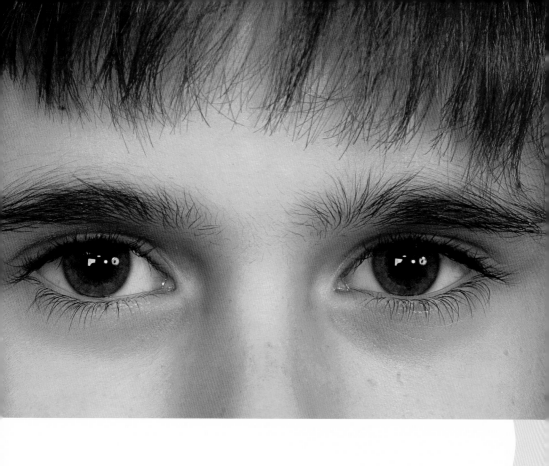

The circle of colour around your pupil is your iris.

In the dark

You can't see very well in the dark...

...but some animals can.

Colours

Your eyes tell you what colour things are.

What colours can you see?

Shapes and sizes

Your eyes tell you the shape of things...

...and how big they are.

Near and far

Your eyes tell you when somebody is near to you...

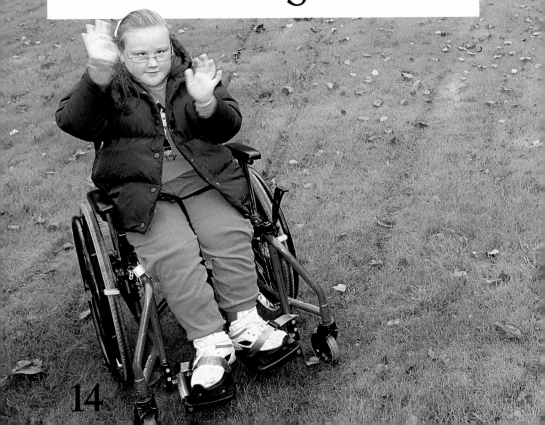

14

...or far away.

Wearing glasses

People who can't see very well wear glasses.

Without glasses, things look blurry.

With glasses, they look clear.

Blindness

Some blind people may use a white cane.

18

Some have a
guide dog.

Protect your eyes

When it is sunny,

we wear a cap...

...or we wear sunglasses to protect our eyes.

21

Using your eyes

Our eyes help us to catch a ball...

22

...or read
a book.

23

Word bank

Look back for these words and pictures.

Blurry

Cane

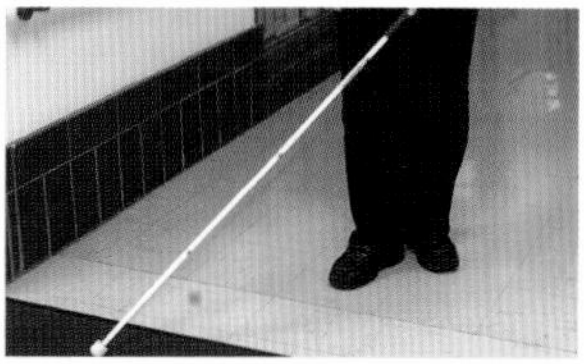

Cap

Colours

Dark

Far

Glasses

Guide dog

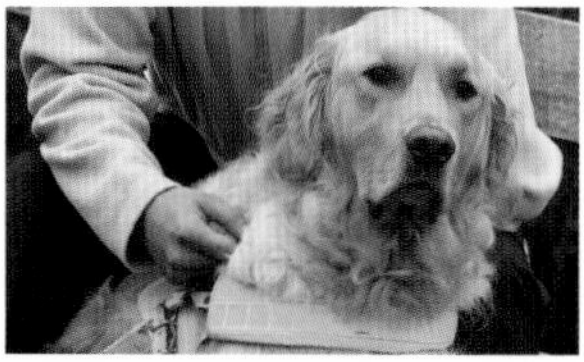

Iris

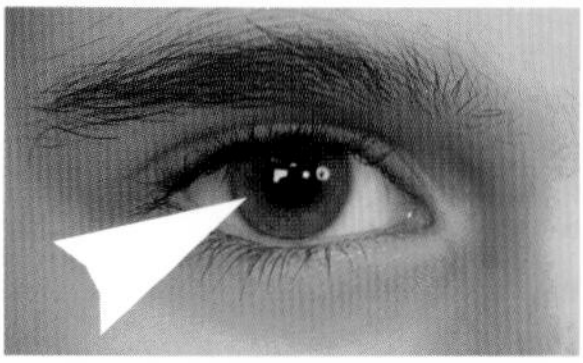

Near

Pupil

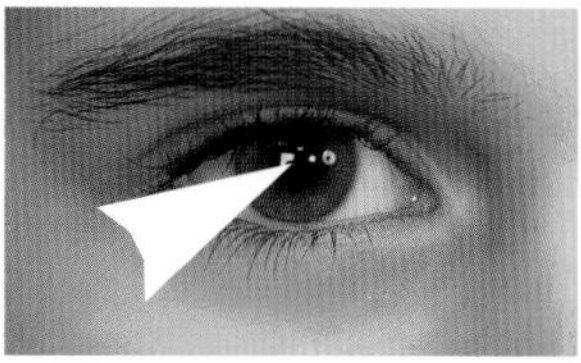

Sunglasses

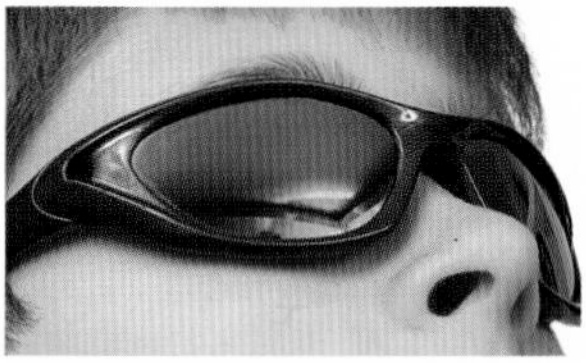

BETTWS

7.6.18